STREET KID

A Creative Non-Fiction Story

ETHEL M. DEVLIN, S.E.J.

PublishAmerica
Baltimore

First printing

At the specific preference of the author, PublishAmerica allowed this work to remain exactly as the author intended, verbatim, without editorial input.

ISBN: 1-4241-2418-2
PUBLISHED BY PUBLISHAMERICA, LLLP
www.publishamerica.com
Baltimore

Printed in the United States of America

Dedication

"Street Kid" is dedicated to my parents, Bert and Mathilda Devlin, in recognition of their years of struggle through the Great Depression. Their hard work and good example have been guiding lights and support for their eight children, myself in particular.

Acknowledgments

Many and sincere thanks to all the kind people, who went out of their way to help get this book published:

Theda Harding, Esther Monk, Kim and Mike Taylor, Virginia Pemberton, Gloria, Chris, Sara and Lovett Harris, Frances Flynn, for providing addresses, phone numbers, pictures and other information;

Dr. Roy Bishop and Ed Coleman for permission to use a wealth of data gleaned from websites:

http://www.valleyweb.com/fundytides,

http://www.town.kentville.ns.ca/kvt/cornwallis.html, respectively;

Frances Crawford for proofreading the manuscripts;

Hugh Atwell, protagonist, for allowing his brain picked repeatedly;

My religious order and natural families and friends for all their support and help;

Charles O. Goulet, author, for suggestions and recommendations regarding printing; Larry Hamel who mediated venues and channels for optimum satisfaction in publishing and marketing the book;

Last but not least, Carmie Devlin, my sister-in-law, without whose typing skills and endless patience, this book would not be.

PROLOGUE

The Prologue to this story is necessary to understand the conditions and circumstances helping to mold and form the boy who became the "Street Kid".

Nova Scotia, like a large bug with swollen abdomen, lies on Canada's eastern coast, in the Atlantic Ocean. It is connected to the province of New Brunswick by a narrow strip of land with water on each side. The narrow strip is called Isthmus of Chignecto. Nova Scotia has numerous rivers and streams, lakes and marshes, rocky highlands and fertile valleys. The most famous waterway is the Bay of Fundy.

Imagine the Atlantic Ocean lying between New Brunswick and the abdomen of the huge bug, Nova Scotia, yet, forcing itself under the wing of the bug, into the Minas Basin. The waters of the Atlantic Ocean, in this area, are known as Bay of Fundy. It has the highest tides on earth reading, at times, 54 feet. If you stood at Cape Split, you would hear the hollow roar of the water filling the Minas Basin, and echoing in the trees growing on the cliffs above. Fourteen billion tons of water slosh into the basin with such force it causes the countryside to bend slightly beneath its weight. This massive phenomena occurs twice every 25 hours and is called high tide.

The opposite of high tide is low tide. The high waters make their way out of the Minas Basin leaving it covered with mud, bearing worms and crustacean, nutritious food for shore birds. Among the shore birds, thousands of sandpipers, migrating to South America, can travel 3 days, non-stop, after feeding on the Minas Basin at low tide.

The waters of the rivers, emptying into the Minas Basin, are pushed against their natural flow by the incoming tide. The effect of the high tide sloshing against the rivers' flow, forms a huge wave called a 'bore'. High tides in river deltas reach a height of 16 feet.

Tourists, amazed at the Fundy's unusual activity, wonder at the many cultures in Nova Scotia. The Mi'Kmaq Indians were the only people at the time the first Europeans inhabited Nova Scotia. They greeted the French colonists at the beginning of the 17th century. The French were called Acadians. They dyked and cultivated the land for agricultural use, planted apple orchards that flourished and produced some of the best apples. There were other fruit but none as renowned as the Annapolis Royal apples. The land occupied by the Acadians stretched from Yarmouth, along the Bay of Fundy, to Grande Pré on the Minas Basin. It included approximately half the large swollen abdomen. This portion of Nova Scotia was called The Land of Evangeline. Evangeline was a symbol of the industrious Acadians, and not a real person. The same land today is called the Annapolis Valley.

In 1755, the Acadians were expelled to England, France, and the New England states. Between 1760 and 1800, the Loyalists, Americans loyal to the British crown, refused to fight in the American Revolution, and fled to Nova Scotia where land awaited them. In 1826 the town of Penook, meaning "fording place", situated on a point of easy crossing on the Cornwallis River, had its name changed to Kentville after Prince Albert, Duke of Kent.

In 1929, depression hit Nova Scotia. Drought, grasshoppers and great poverty struck most of North America. Families scrimped and scrounged to make ends meet. Nothing was wasted. Parents worked long hours and took advantage of every opportunity to earn a wage or to trade extras for necessities. Nova Scotia had fish and fruit in abundance. These were exchanged for flour, sugar, spices, medication or fuel. Children wore hand-me-downs or makeovers. Mothers were adept at turning flour and sugar bags into tea towels, sheets, pillowcases and embroidered table linen. Some made lingerie from the same sturdy cotton. Children pitched in to help their parents during summer vacations. They picked and sold wild berries to buy school supplies in the fall. Depression years brought deflation. Movies were 10 cents, chocolate bars, five cents, B.B. Bats, long caramel suckers, were two cents. An apple or tomato sold for one or two cents, depending on the size.

The depression continued into the 1930's, years referred to as the "Dirty Thirties". In 1939 World War Two broke out. The war raged in Europe until 1945. Money, metal, food and commodities were sent overseas for the thousands of Canadians fighting there. The effects of the depression and the war kept Canada in a state of poverty until 1950.

CHAPTER 1

In 1928, Hugh Atwell was born. His ancestors emigrated from Connecticut to settle in Nova Scotia in 1760. They originated in England and Ireland and were known as builders. They acquired dykeland, timberland and a sawmill in Nova Scotia. With the land and the mill, the family was able to pursue its trade.

Walter Atwell, Hugh's father, chose to live in New Minas and rented a house there. Hugh was born in Gaspereau, before the family moved to New Minas. His father was a construction worker. He was building a house in Aldershot, three or four miles from New Minas. He left for work early each morning, returning after dark, and walking the round trip carrying his tools for work. He planned to move his family to Aldershot because the house in New Minas was not completed and could lead to accidents. The rafters for the ceiling were bare. Tiger, Hugh's cat, liked to climb out on the rafters. That was fine until young Hugh crawled through an opening at the top of the stairs, thinking he would rescue the cat. Dorothy Atwell, Hugh's mother, got her son down, and had the opening nailed shut before an accident occurred. Dorothy was pregnant. She got the two older boys, Asie, age nine, and Dempsey, age seven, fed and off to school. Hugh was five and Avery was three. Dorothy did not feel well and prayed the baby would not come early. She lost three boys since her marriage to Walter. The thought of those three children made her sad. She started preparing breakfast to get her mind on happier times. As the oatmeal cooked, Dorothy washed and dressed her two small boys.

"The day is beautiful," she said as she buttoned shirts and tied laces, "a little walk after breakfast will do us all a world of good."

Hugh picked up his cat, Tiger, and told him about the walk. Tiger, as usual, wasn't impressed, but he trotted out the door behind Hugh as the trio set out. The air was fresh and brisk. A slight breeze came up but the warmth of the sun kept the cold in check. As they ambled along, Mother spoke about the many gifts God gives us each day; the sunbeams to cheer and warm us, the fresh air for breathing, the water for making plants grow, the trees and plants to enjoy, to eat or to use for building things.

Hugh listened and looked at everything as his mom spoke. He asked, "Mom, where is God?"

"God is in Heaven with the angels, Hugh," answered Mom, "but He is also with all of us, and someday we will join the angels," continued Mom.

Later in the day, Hugh thought about joining the angels. He told Tiger, "You, too, can join the angels. We might play tag or run a race with them," he said. "Would you like to join the angels, Tiger?"

Tiger answered by jumping from Hugh's arms. He headed for the stove, found a warm spot on the rug behind the stove, stretched out, and fell asleep.

Mother smiled at her son's comments to the cat. She had a special place in her heart for Hugh. He was a stocky child, with pleasing personality, laughing eyes and a ready smile for everyone he met. Dorothy thought he was destined to do something special.

Perhaps its because he's so sensitive about others feelings, she thought.

Dorothy's thoughts were interrupted as sharp pains wracked her body and made her cry out. Walter had entered the house and hearing the cry, hurried into the living room. Dorothy, pale and shaken, told him she should go to the birthing house right away. Walter was worried. He called the birthing house in Kentville and tried to get Doctor Bishop, but the doctor was out of town. Walter called the neighbor, a car owner, who said he'd be in front of Walter's house in two minutes. Walter helped Dorothy into the car, then, got in himself. The trip to Kentville took 20 minutes.

Asie and Dempsey walked into the house while Father was calling the birth house. Neither boy understood what was happening until the car left with their parents, then, they realized Mom was going to have a baby.

Dad returned with the owner of the car. He called the boys together, took the two small boys on his knees and tried to explain to the four that Mom's life was in grave danger.

"Mom is very sick," he said. "She will be away until she gets better. I want you to do all your chores and schoolwork. We'll try to keep the house clean while she's away. Now, there is a family living about 4 miles from here. They'd like Avery to live with them for a while. They have a small dog and farm animals. It's very kind of them to offer and Avery will be happy there." So it happened.

CHAPTER 2

Father was talking to his children when the phone rang. As he listened, a sob escaped from deep inside. The boys gathered around him as he said,

"Your mother and little brother could not be saved. Both are gone. The women at the birthing house did all they could but Mom slipped away before the doctor arrived."

Asie and Dempsey had some understanding of death; Hugh and Avery never heard about it. Hugh expected Mother back. He was certain she would be in bed when he and Tiger awoke in the morning. He would carry Tiger to Mom's bed, slip his feet under the blanket then, slide down beside her. She would say,

"All right; go back to sleep you two."

There was no one in bed when Hugh and Tiger entered Mom's room. Avery's crib was also empty and everything was quiet. Puzzled, Hugh went back to his bed. He sat cross-legged wondering where Mom could be.

She went away in the car but didn't come back. Where could she be?

Hugh sat there for a long time, dazed. He dressed in the clothes on the chair beside his bed, then made his way to the kitchen. He ate the slice of bread and jam and drank the milk left on the table at his place. Tiger came out from behind the stove. He walked round and round Hugh, rubbing his head and neck on the child's legs. Hugh didn't seem to notice Tiger. After eating he went to his room and sat on his bed again, as thoughts of Mom went round and round in his head. Hugh did not notice how sleepy he was. His head dropped sideways and his body followed. Soon he was fast asleep.

Hugh was awakened by the warm sun beaming through the window. He got up, put on his jacket, and went outside. He looked at the trees, the plants and the sky. He felt a gentle breeze in his hair and the warmth of the sun on his face.

God gave them to us, he said half aloud. *Where is Mom?* he cried. Hugh made his way behind the house so as not to be seen. No one looked for him nor called for him. *I need Mom. Oh Mom! Where are you?* Overcome by loneliness and grief, Hugh crumpled to the ground where he sobbed, consoled by no one. He stopped crying and sat up. Father found him.

"Hugh, you've been crying. Tell me about it." So saying, he picked up the boy and carried him to a shady spot where he sat with the child on his knee.

"Where is Mom?" questioned Hugh.

"She's gone, Hugh," answered his dad.

"Where did she go?" asked the youngster.

"She's gone to Heaven, Hugh."

"Well, when is she coming back?" Hugh persisted. Walter Atwell pressed the boy to his heart as he fought back his tears.

"Hugh, Mom died. She's with the Angels in Heaven. She won't be coming back but she'll watch over you. She'll be near you but you won't see her. You can talk to her and she'll listen. You'll know in your heart she's with you. She'll help you if you have problems."

A picture of Mom sprang to Hugh's imagination, a picture of Mom with angel wings and a shiny halo over her hair. From that day, and even today, Hugh turned toward his angel mother for help. As he got older, his understanding of God's loving care grew from his memory of his mom. He called on her when there was no one to turn to. Somehow, an answer came and the answer seemed right. As Hugh grew from toddler to teen he kept his mom busy running his errands. She never failed him.

CHAPTER 3

Dorothy Atwell had gone to heaven. Her body had been laid to rest in the cemetery in New Minas. The funeral was described by an elderly lady, "The saddest sight! Those four young boys without a mother! What will the poor father do?" After the burial, the community gathered in the church hall for lunch.

Walter stepped to the front of the room, and surprised everyone with an announcement and request,

"I've completed my house in Aldershot. I hope to move into my own home in a couple of months. I'm grateful to all you kind neighbors for coming to the funeral and to those who've offered to transport furniture and house wares with wagons and buggies when the moving date is set. I am most grateful to the families willing to prepare meals for my family. Your kindness touches me deeply."

Walter stopped to wipe his eyes and blow his nose. The families lingered long enough to assure Walter they would be back to help with the moving, as soon as he gave the word.

A month after the funeral, a flatbed pulled by a team of Clydesdale, rolled in beside the Atwell house in New Minas. Men unloaded three empty barrels. The ladies were busy wrapping chinaware and glassware in sheets and towels. They placed them in the barrels along with the children's clothing. As each room was emptied of its contents, the ladies gave it a good sweeping, washed the windows, and scrubbed the floors. Each room, in turn, had its contents packed and furniture removed before it was cleaned. The men carried the packed barrels and heavy articles to the flatbed and buggies. They wasted no time. Soon, the Atwell's possessions were ready to be transported to Aldershot.

A family of three went ahead to make Walter's new house ready and inviting. They picked a bunch of Mayflowers to put on the table, when it arrived. They also brought a kettle of soup and boxes of sandwiches to feed the hungry workers.

Walter Atwell was the last to arrive at his new home. He stayed behind in New Minas to check the house and yard and return the key to the owner. Satisfied with the work and state of the place, Walter untethered the horse left for his use, and hitched it to the buggy. It took half an hour to trot the horse to Aldershot to join the group awaiting his arrival.

Several families in the community of Aldershot organized a round robin program for helping the Atwell family. Each family signed a list stating their preferred day for cooking, mending and cleaning. The children had good care by neighbors, from the time Dorothy passed away, until Walter got a live-in lady toward the end of 1933. The lady was Viola Acker. She arrived with her toddler son, Gordon.

Hugh started school at age six and a half. He liked his teacher and he liked learning to read, write, and solve arithmetic problems. He learned sounds of the alphabet rather than their names, and surprised himself reading words by sounding them. Sounding made reading slow at first, but served as a good background for reading well.

Hugh thought the grade one primer boring. Most of the words had four letters. For example, he read in Dick and Jane:

Dick is a boy.
Jane is a girl.
Come, Dick, come.
Come, Jane, come.
Or again;
Spot is a dog.
Puff is a cat.
Run, Spot, run.
Jump, Puff, jump.

Hugh shared his thoughts about the boring books. He shared his ideas and opinions with his school pals. As his mind developed, his relationship with friends and teachers grew and improved. Early in the school year, he rushed home to Tiger after school. A month or so later he hurried home to speak to the lady who cooked his meals, sewed buttons on his shirts or darned the toes and heels of his socks.

I wish she'd live with us, forever, mused Hugh. *Asie isn't as bossy! I hate it when he slaps my face, just to make me cry.*

Walter married Viola on November ninth, 1935. A little girl, Shirley, was born to the couple. Two years later Viola had to be admitted to a hospital. Her head gave her unbearable pain. Doctors discovered an inoperable tumor on her brain. They were unable to help her.

In 1937, Hugh was nine. Walter's work took him away from home most days. He decided to put 14 year old Asie in charge while he was away. Walter did not realize the amount of hostility between Asie and Hugh. Asie exercised his authority by slapping Hugh in the face. Hugh was quick and strong and promised to get even with him. The opportunity came and Hugh took it.

CHAPTER 4

Hugh Atwell, stocky 10 year old, with light colored hair, frightened brown eyes, and worried face, stood hidden at the corner of the house. He watched a neighbor lift Asie, bleeding and stunned from the two-by-four Hugh used in revenge.

I didn't mean to hurt him, only wanted to get back at him for slapping my face to make me cry. Tears blurred Hugh's vision as he thought of his mother's death. *Mom, help me,* he breathed, wiping his eyes. Crouched low, he headed for the neighbor's barn. *I have to leave, can't stay here anymore. I'll sleep in the loft and leave early, before I'm missed.* Thought's of Asie's bullying raced in Hugh's head. Darkness made him edgy and fearful. *What will become of me?* Something brushed by his face and snuggled beside him. It was Tiger. Hugh slept.

A train, racing through Aldershot awakened Hugh. He jumped up and headed for the ladder. Dawn was breaking.

Better take something for breakfast, he thought, as he tiptoed into the house. He stuffed two apples, a few doughnuts, and an orange into a bag, then, retraced his steps out the door. He felt Tiger at his heels. A knot caught in his throat as he whispered, "You can't come, Tiger. Go away!"

I won't take Tiger. He'd have nowhere to go and nothing to eat. Hugh's eyes filled with tears, but he brushed them off and ran toward the shelter of the trees along the road leading to Kentville. *It's good the apple trees are blooming; I can hide under their bent branches so people approaching wouldn't notice me.* Casting his eyes to right and left, he checked lest someone was coming. *Running away is awful. What else can I do?* he wondered. *Oh, Mom! Make sure Asie doesn't die.* Hugh's heart was filled with fear as one sad thought followed another.

Approaching Kentville, not three miles from Aldershot, Hugh stopped long enough to get his bearings. Ducking in and out among the houses, he made his way to the laundromat where he'd seen boxes stacked. He selected a large one, placed the open end over a hot air vent and crawled inside. With his legs stretched toward the heat, Hugh ate the provisions from home. Everything was tasty and filled his stomach. The food made him drowsy and he slept soundly. Waking with a start, he jumped out of the box thinking, *I'll look for empties so I can buy supper.*

The sun was high. Bottles were easy to find, tossed anywhere by careless users. They'd sell for one or two cents, depending on size. Hugh made 36 cents. Clutching his money, he headed for the store beside the barbershop. Two boys stood scowling at him. The bigger one stuck out his foot to trip him; the smaller one gave him a push. Hugh's clenched fist sent the first boy sprawling; the other boy disappeared. *Dad told me never to pick fights, but if I was forced into it, I should fight hard and fast. I was forced by those two,* he figured.

A week later, Hugh decided to go fishing in The Old Mill Stream in East Kentville. *Wow! Look at those beauties, like tiny salmon.* Breaking off a flat, leafy ash branch, he slipped it under the fish and flipped two smelt onto the grassy shore. He arranged rocks in a small circle, filled the center with dry leaves, twigs and sticks, then lit them with a match from his pocket. Impaling the fish on a long stick, he held them over the fire while they cooked. The fish were delicious and filling to the hungry youngster. He, then, poured water over the embers and kicked sand over the scraps before returning to his box.

Getting cleaned up was a problem for Hugh. The days were cool making it difficult to wash in the stream. *Why not use the station washroom?* thought Hugh. *I'll slip in while the guard is checking tracks.* When he woke in the morning, Hugh crawled out of his cardboard shelter, stretched his cramped legs and hurried to the station for a quick wash, making sure he wiped out the basin and put paper towels in the waste. The guard feigned not to see the urchin as he came and went.

The business people of Kentville watched out for the street kid. Mr. Lenihan, the restaurant and rooming house owner, beckoned Hugh from the street.

"Have you had your breakfast, kid? Take your hat off and go to the kitchen. Mrs. Barnaby wants to see you."

Mrs. Barnaby, the cook, set a heaping plate of food before Hugh, then, sat back to watch him enjoy it. Hugh lingered over the large wedge of apple pie, trying to make it last forever. He thanked the cook, then offered to run errands or do chores for Mr. Lenihan.

The movie theater manager occasionally gave Hugh tickets to the movies. He reprimanded him if he sneaked into the theater without a ticket. His admonitions were gentle and respectful. Hugh learned respect from the man's kindness.

Hugh liked to hang around Mr. Joseph's pool hall. The kid was a pool shark, men loved to challenge. His adept handling of the cue brought smiles to their faces. They'd bring him a sandwich or share the one they'd brought for themselves. Hugh played for the house. He found pleasure in his ability to get the better of his competitors and seized every opportunity to exercise his standing invitation to drop in anytime.

If Hugh was hungry and had no money for food, he took carrots from gardens and apples from orchards. The owners ignored the hungry boy's thefts. "I could not deprive a child of food," was the usual comment.

As the sun set in the evening, and darkness crept across the town of Kentville, Hugh felt alone and afraid. He crawled into his cardboard box and covered himself with a blanket left in the laundromat. Deep sobs arose from the child's soul. He spoke to his angel mother and asked her to stay near. As peaceful calm descended upon him, he slept. In the morning, he folded his box, as was his custom, and inserted it between the laundry wall foundation and a garbage disposal bin. The laundry roof overhang protected the space from wind and rain and kept the box dry.

CHAPTER 5

Two ladies from England, came to live in Kentville. They had substantial financial means and procured a fine mansion on Main Street, across from the Anglican Church. They hired several men and women as gardeners, chauffeur, cook and housekeeper. The ladies were Mrs. Botsford and Mrs. Chipman. They were sensitive and sympathetic toward persons less fortunate than they. Hearing from Peter Cleyle about the street kid, one of the ladies, Mrs. Botsford, went to see the clothier.

Hugh had been on the street a few months. His clothes were worn and tattered. Half the sole of one shoe was gone, as though eaten by rodents. Mr. Cleyle asked, "Where do you live, Hugh?"

"Over there, by the laundry," answered Hugh.

"Come in for a minute, I've got shoes that might fit you." He led Hugh to the shoe department and fitted him with a pair of sturdy shoes and a pair of socks. Hugh, awed by Peter Cleyle's generosity, welcomed both gifts.

"Best shoes I've ever had. Thank you, sir," observed Hugh.

Mr. Cleyle then led Hugh to the boys' wear and outfitted him with a shirt, trousers, shorts and tee shirt. The boy's eyes opened wide. He was awestruck for words.

"Always wear shorts and a tee shirt next to your skin. They will absorb sweat and spare you embarrassment."

Hugh remembered Mr. Cleyle's wise words through the years. He was overwhelmed by the kindness shown to him and speaks of it almost 70 years later.

Hugh found out the name of his benefactress while on a leave from the army. He recalled how the ladies from the mansion, after visiting Peter Cleyle at his store, sent him a message, through Peter. They wanted to see the boy.

"Oh, boy! I'm going to their big house!" exclaimed Hugh as he walked beside Peter, toward the mansion on Main Street.

The housekeeper answered the doorbell and admitted the two guests to a sunny parlor. Hugh looked about, then craned his neck around the doorframe. He saw a beautiful curved stairway leading to a second floor. His jaw dropped as he gazed at the elegant drapes, the hand-carved newel, and above, a crystal chandelier. He couldn't believe any home could be as beautiful.

Angel Mom, this place looks like heaven, he mused.

The cook cut in on Hugh's thoughts to announce, "Tea is served."

Hugh stood close to Peter Cleyle. He'd copy his movements and choices at table. As the pair entered the dining hall, Hugh saw the two ladies. He surmised from their attire, they were the owners and immediately blurted out, "What a beautiful house! You must be rich! Where did you get all the money?"

The ladies smiled as the exclamations and questions tumbled out.

"We brought it from England, Hugh. Our husbands were bankers. There were rumors of a great war. Our husbands insisted we come to Canada. We love this country and the peaceful town of Kentville. Our husbands will come after the trouble is over. Now, let's have tea."

Tea over, Mrs. Botsford told Hugh there would be a quarter left, every Saturday, in the small tin box at the base of the fountain. It would be his to use as he wished.

Mr. Rose was head of the Children's Aid Society in Kentville. Mrs. Botsford turned to him to find a good home for Hugh. She was willing to pay for Hugh's room and board if a suitable home could be found. She did not want the child to be a ward of the government. Hugh impressed Mrs. Botsford with his intelligence and curiosity. She knew the Atwell family and the tough times they had experienced. She wanted to help, but on her terms. Her terms meant letting the boy think Children's Aid was responsible for his upkeep.

Hugh Atwell is now 76 years. He ponders on his childhood and muses, *The people of Kentville were so kind toward me! What would have become of me on the street? Thinking of those years fills me with gratitude.*

CHAPTER 6

Hugh, tired of being alone, cold and hungry, wondered where he would find food. It was a frosty autumn day in 1939. He had been on the streets of Kentville, Nova Scotia, for a year and a half. Hunger gnawed at his empty stomach. Memories of the beating he gave his older brother troubled him. He thought of his mother in heaven. He needed her protection. His heart cried out, *Mom, Mom, Help me!* The thought of his mother calmed him.

Hugh walked to the grocery store and peered into the big window on his way to the door. The sight of 30 or more people checked his impulse to enter. He hesitated. The gnawing inside him increased, making him feel faint. *What should I do?* Mother's image rose in his mind, boosting his courage, and he entered the store.

A large wheel of Gouda cheese, cut into wedges of varying sizes, lay on a butcher table at the far end of a long counter. Customers selecting a week's supply of groceries, paid no attention to Hugh, as he stared at the cheese. With a sudden swoop, he seized a pound wedge, slipped it under his jacket and walked out the store. The grocer saw the boy take the cheese, but made no attempt to stop him.

Outside, Hugh broke into a run, dodging and ducking behind buildings to get back to the laundry without being seen. He stopped abruptly before the spot he kept his box. The space was empty. No other large box was in sight. Undaunted, Hugh turned and headed for the

Cornwallis Bridge. He had seen a number of abandoned cars. One old Buick had soft seats and an intact rear window. Hugh crawled into the back, pulled the cheese from under his jacket and started eating. He did not stop until the cheese had disappeared, then he fell asleep.

Police Chief, John Brown, a gigantic man with a heart of gold, and disposition to match, cruised over the bridge and down Cornwallis Street. The weather turned bitter. The Chief did not want drunks sleeping out on such a night. They prowled about the parking area in search of shelter. The lights of the police cruiser caught a slight movement in the old Buick. The car stopped abruptly and the chief hurried to the car. He flashed his torch on to a young kid holding his stomach and groaning.

Hugh awoke from his sleep in great pain. His stomach felt hard, sweat poured over his body. He thought he would die. Deep inside he cried out *Mom, help! I'm dying, Mom, Mom!*

A light beamed. Hugh grew afraid and quiet. A voice called,

"Hugh, what is the matter? Are you sick?"

"I'm dying, Sir, I'm dying," moaned Hugh. The policeman gently gathered Hugh in his arms, placed him in the cruiser, then, drove to the jailhouse. He had the jailer take the boy to the staff section and he, John Brown, called Dr. Bishop.

The kind doctor probed the hurting stomach and belly.

"What did you have for supper?" he asked.

"Cheese," answered Hugh.

The doctor gave Hugh an enema. The kid was embarrassed and squeamish during the procedure, but, relieved and freed once his body functions kicked in. He felt fine, grew drowsy, and was asleep in a couple of minutes. He woke after 10 the next morning to find Chief of Police, Brown, seated beside his bed.

"Hugh, you and I have to talk," began the chief.

Just my chance to come clean, thought Hugh. Then aloud, "Sir, I want to tell you something. I took the cheese at the grocery store without paying for it. I had no money. I was awful hungry, Sir." I'll find lots of bottles and pay for the cheese. I'm sorry, Sir."

Tears burned behind the chief's eyes. He rose and walked to the window. He thought, *This child has suffered too much!* His emotions checked, he turned to Hugh saying, "Stealing is not right, young man, but you did not steal. You needed food. The cheese was the food you needed."

Gee! He's not mad at me, mused Hugh, as he breathed a sigh of relief. The lawman's words broke in on his thoughts.

"Mr. Rose knows of a good family in Lower Wolfville. They've had two foster children for some time and want another boy about your age. Think about that, Hugh. You'd go to school, help on the farm, and have a kind and caring family to support you. They are the Rays, Len and Lena, a young married couple with no children. Lena and Len will see that you have food, clean clothes, a bed to sleep on and a place to get cleaned up."

The mention of Mr. Rose reinforced Hugh's certainty he would become a ward of the government. He didn't want to be a ward but he would have food and shelter. The thought of having a bed to sleep in, elated him. *Will I get used to having space to move, turn over, pull my knees up to keep warm?* he wondered. *A mom to care for me, to listen to me! I could whoop and shout, but, I better not. Angel Mom, I don't know if I'm dreaming. I love you, Mom!* he added.

"Sir, I want to go to school. I'll be older than the others but I'll work hard to get ahead. I know I'll love the Rays. I need a family. They'll be right for me, I know. When will I go? asked Hugh.

"Mr. Rose will take you this afternoon. He mentioned he'd be back in Kentville around one. He'll take you to Lower Wolfville and introduce you to the Rays."

So it happened. Hugh, dressed in the clothes given him by Mr. Cleyle, with no suitcase or bag, hopped into Mr. Rose's Model T and set out to begin a new life with a family he did not know. He felt safe knowing his angel mother was by his side. On the way, Mr. Rose chatted with Hugh. His patient understanding and gentle attitude dispelled the butterflies of anxiety fighting for control in the kid's stomach.

"Look, Hugh! See the brown house with white trim sitting on a small farm? That property belongs to the Rays."

As Hugh scanned the countryside, he saw a barn, sheds, a brown house with white trim, and several farm animals. He liked the place! *I know I'll like the Rays,* he thought, *and I hope they will like me.* Hugh's thoughts raced in his head, his heart fluttered a little as he said, "I'm, ready, Mr. Rose."

CHAPTER 7

An unforgettable whiff of fresh bread wafted around Hugh's nose as he walked to the Ray's door beside Mr. Rose. Len and Lena stepped onto the stoop to welcome the young boy who stood there looking scared.

"I'm Len and this is Lena," offered the young man. "Come in, Hugh! Meet Virginia and Lawrence. They've been with us for a while." Hugh aged 11, smiled and relaxed as an eight year old girl and 10 year old boy stepped forward. A muted understanding appeared on the faces of the three youngsters as shy smiles lit their eyes.

"Why don't you two show Hugh around the house and farm? Lena will call when dinner's ready."

Mr. Rose, standing below the stoop, came into the house to complete arrangements for Hugh's upkeep with the Rays. He delivered payment for three months, as instructed by Mrs. Botsford, and explained the next payments would be mailed to them. Mr. Rose left, sensing Hugh would be happy, and feel comfortable at home in his new family. Virginia and Lawrence showed their new friend the room he'd share with Lawrence. The sight of a bed, after sleeping in a box or old car a year and a half, stunned Hugh. *Angel Mom, thank you,* he whispered in his mind. *Can't wait to try it out.*

"Your bed is by the wall; this one's mine," instructed Lawrence.

"That's swell!" commented Hugh.

Lena entered the room stating, "Dinner's ready. I've set your place beside Lawrence, Hugh!"

"Thanks, Mrs. Ray," answered Hugh.

"You may call us Len and Lena, Hugh. We are both young and prefer our given names."

The image of the bed, for his use, popped time and time again in Hugh's mind. *If I do go to sleep, I might not wake up,* he thought. *Angel Mom, please push bedtime closer.*

No one woke Hugh from his first night of blissful sleep at the Ray's. The sunbeams on his face roused him at 10:30. He got up, climbed into the blue overalls Lena placed on the chair beside his bed and slipped into a checked red shirt hanging on the back of the chair. *I like these,* he thought as he checked the bib and pants' pockets. *They are like farm kids' clothes. I like 'em.*

Len heard footsteps in Hugh's room and called the boy.

"We left you some rolled oats, Hugh. Come have a bite to eat. I've got chores lined up for you."

Hugh ate a hearty breakfast of cereal, eggs, toast and milk, and declared "I'm ready to work."

"Your first chore is to give the calf a quart of milk. I have the milk in a pail in the kitchen from this morning's milking. Stick your hand in the milk and move your fingers. The calf will suck on them and drink milk as well."

"Sounds easy," commented Hugh.

"Wear my old bib overalls over yours. Calves can be sloppy. You'll find the overalls hanging inside the barn door."

Hugh picked up the calf's pail, headed for the barn and stepped into Len's old bibs. The calf watched him approach the coral and blatted.

"Come on, boy," coaxed Hugh, as he neared the bull calf.

The calf had other ideas. He put his head into the pail, butted it, and sent Hugh sprawling. The boy was not deterred. After several unsuccessful attempts to get the calf to drink, he grabbed the strap around its neck and jumped on its back. The calf bucked as he ran, throwing Hugh off to the side. Hugh clung to the neck strap and found himself under the belly of the calf. Hugh's outer overalls were large and as the calf ran, it stepped on the crotch of the pants. Hugh was dragged through mud, mire and manure, until the calf stopped, exhausted. Hugh removed Len's sorry-looking overalls and left them on the top of Lena's mending basket. He had sore spots from being dragged, but was able to laugh with the Rays over his first farm experience.

Neighbors of the Rays raised potatoes, acres of potatoes, for commercial use. Local children, 12 years or more, were encouraged to help in planting and picking potatoes to earn money for family or personal needs. Hugh kept his ears and eyes alerted to jobs offering money, and was among the first to apply. His hard work at picking, planting, haying, or other jobs, landed him many opportunities to make money.

I got $1.05 for picking potatoes. Movies are five cents. I'll take someone to the theatre on Saturday, thought Hugh as he whistled his way to the coal bin. One of his jobs was to haul a hod of coal to the kitchen for Lena's cooking. He had two hours before the movie started. *I'll split kindling and see if Grandpa is using the horses today.* Grandpa and Grandma Ray lived on Len and Lena's property. They had two Children's Aid boys, Teddy and Clarence. Grandpa asked Hugh to harness the horses and drive him to the hayfield. Teddy and Clarence resented Grandpa calling on Hugh to help, but, when he did, a fight ensued between Hugh and the boys. Once, when Grandpa went to town, Teddy and Clarence decided to beat up on Hugh. They found him in the lane talking softly to the horses. Teddy administered the first blow. Hugh came back at him with a right upper cut, knocking him out cold. Both, Teddy and Clarence, were down when Hugh fled from the Ray's farm. The tide was out and he hid under the muddy clod overhang along the bank of the Cornwallis River. The Rays, returning from their trip to Wolfville, saw him from a rise in the road but were unable to locate him as they approached the spot. They called and searched, then feigned a retreat. Hugh thought they'd left and came out from his hideaway. They spoke to him kindly.

"Don't be afraid. Nothing is so bad it can't be fixed. Come along, Hugh."

A meeting was called after the beating incident. It was attended by

Grandpa and Grandma, Len and Lena, and the five children.

"What can be done to avoid fights and misunderstandings in the future?" asked Lena Ray.

A five minute period of silence gave each person present time to think.

Grandpa broke the silence with a solution he thought would work.

"I don't like fights and I don't think anyone likes them. If something is not right, or you think it's not right, tell an adult. Grandma, Len, Lena or myself, one of us will help you clear it up before it gets worse."

"Sounds good to me," piped Virginia, "I don't like fights either."

The boys looked at one another. Teddy extended his hand to Hugh. The two shook hands as both said, "I'm sorry." Clarence admitted he should not have egged Teddy on. A stronger friendship developed among the boys and with Lawrence and Virginia.

Hugh thought of his mother. *Mom, will I ever be able to walk away from provocation?*

CHAPTER 8

Hugh was faced with one more volatile situation during the time spent with the Rays. A cute little blond girl named Helen Mohar, caught his attention. She sat in a desk opposite to him in school. He had never taken a girl to the movies. He wrote her a note: "Helen, will you go to the movies with me on Saturday?" and passed it near the opened book she was reading. He sat back and waited. A tiny square of paper held one word in answer, "YES." Hugh smiled.

The school bully, Andrew, claimed Helen Mohar as his girlfriend, but Helen had no interest in him. On the day planned, Hugh and Helen got their tickets, then selected two adjoining seats halfway down the theater's middle aisle. They became engrossed in the Western movie and did not notice the bully keeping them in his sight. As the pair left the theatre, they passed a door leading to an upstairs apartment. Andrew guessed they would pass there and as they did, he fell upon Hugh's back and started choking him. Hugh executed a rapid forward thrust of his body, landing his opponent on his back. Provoked to anger, Hugh began pummeling his assailant. His blows could have maimed Andrew, had not two gentlemen separated the boys.

Hugh's thoughts were on the fight he'd had with Andrew. *Angel Mom, I don't know why I fight. Well, I know I was defending myself, and Helen too, but why am I always getting into fights? Help me, Mom, show me some other way.*

Hugh forgot about the fight as he walked along the Bay of Fundy at low tide. He noted a path made by numerous muskrats. *I'll trap them,* he planned, *skin them and sell the pelts. Len has three muskrat traps he'll let me use. In no time money will roll in.* He increased his speed and got back to the Rays earlier than usual. He cleaned the traps in preparation for the morrow.

At dawn, Hugh hurried along the muskrat trail, dug in the mud to set his traps, and dreamed of becoming rich. The position of the sun warned him to run before the school bell rang. After school he'd whittle flat forms for the pelts. Each trap held a dead muskrat. They were skinned behind the manure pile and the carcasses buried therein. The hides were turned inside out and stretched over a form to dry. At the end of the first week of trapping, Hugh had 11 pelts. He would let Len in on his secret.

Hugh brought the dried pelts, neatly piled and tied with binder twine, and lay them before Len, as he mended the harness.

"What have we here!" exclaimed Len.

"Muskrat pelts, I prepared," answered Hugh.

"These are ship rats, Hugh." laughed Len. "You did a great job of stretching and drying them but they are useless in the market." Hugh was surprised but not crestfallen. He began laughing along with Len.

Oh, Mom, that was a boo boo, but now I know what's what.

Toward the end of June, Len and Lena called a meeting with the children. Hugh was 13, Lawrence 12, and Virginia 10. They wondered what the problem could be.

"We've called this meeting to let you know we won't be boarding any children next year, nor any year, for that matter. We'll miss all of you and would like to have you stay on. Our desire is to have a family of our own. We can't have two families. We're telling you before school is out so you will have time to think about where you'd like to live in the fall. Mr. Rose will be in soon and you can talk to him if you have preferences."

The three children were sad to leave the Rays. Hugh liked Len and Lena and loved to be one of their family. He wanted to live with them until he finished school. It was not to be.

What will I do? he wondered. It took a week to decide he'd return to the home he fled in 1938. So it happened.

CHAPTER 9

Silence greeted Hugh as he opened the door to his childhood home. No one was about. Memories of the day he fled, flooded his mind and tears rolled down his cheeks. *Mom! Are you with me, Mom?* cried his anguished soul. He did not move, but stood transfixed, hand on door knob, one foot on the threshold. A moment passed, then, as though in answer to his mother's touch, Hugh's body relaxed and he walked into the house.

Nothing seemed to have changed since that fated day in 1938. The table stood in its usual central place, four chairs pushed against its sides and a fifth pulled out, awaiting the return of the head of the family. Beyond the table, Hugh noted no changes in the kitchen. He turned toward the staircase leading to his bedroom. His bed, stripped to the mattress and covered with a light afghan, seemed bare and cold. As he stood staring at it, an image of a five year old sitting cross-legged on the bed, rocking back and forth, forced him to live anew the pain of his mother's death. Unlike that day in 1933, a sense of peace enwrapped him, making Hugh aware of Mom's protective care. *I love you, Mom* he smiled gratefully.

Hugh stood before the room window as thoughts of his family entered his mind. Dad was at work, as usual. He would return after dark carrying his tools, weary after a long day. Asie, a dispatch rider in the army, awaited his unit's transfer to Italy. He received several stars and medals during active service in Britain, France, Germany, Italy and Africa. Dempsey lived in Gaspereau with relatives. At 17, he joined the army specializing in the use of heavy mounted guns and became an artillery man. Avery was with the family who took him when Mom died. Shirley, Hugh's half sister, lived with a family in Avonport.

With everyone but father living away from home, Hugh had no one to turn to. *Its best I go to school, get my grade six,* he decided.

No one woke him in the morning; there was no breakfast, no clean shirt to wear. Hugh's resolve, to get ahead in school, was short lived. He needed support and encouragement, such as he received from the Rays; without that help, Hugh's attendance dropped as did his grades. The Non Permanent Army Militia recruited men to train as Privates in the West Nova Scotia Regiment. Hugh joined up in 1942 giving his age as 18. He served from February 1942 to March 1943. A month after his fifteenth birthday, Hugh joined the army. He needed to have his birth certificate altered by a professional, to make it look "real" so he went to have a chat with Ethel, secretary to a lawyer. He had a crush on Ethel.

I can't tell her I love her, she's 4 years older and has a boyfriend, but if I'm accepted, she'll be impressed. So thinking, Hugh approached the secretary.

"I'm impressed you want to fight for your country, Hugh. You're fifteen! You're too young to die," commented Ethel. Hugh did not answer but he thought, *what kind of life do I lead: no prepared meals, no one to turn to for help and guidance, no one who seems to care what becomes of me.*

He answered Ethel, "It will be easier to fight for my country than to wander aimlessly, as I do."

Ethel typed Hugh's birth date to read February 7, 1925. "Take care, Hugh," she said as he took the certificate from her.

"Thank you, Miss," beamed a grateful Hugh, as he walked out the lawyer's office and into the tattoo parlor to have Ethel's name tattooed above his left wrist. *I'll be forever grateful to you, Miss Ethel,* he mused, *forever grateful.*

CHAPTER 10

Halifax had a medical center where men enlisted for service. An army car took Hugh and other young men to Halifax. There an officer ordered Hugh to get a brush cut and complete physical checkup. Satisfied Hugh was a healthy man, a medical officer had a kit issued containing seasonal clothing and personal hygiene articles. Hugh was detailed to Aldershot for basic training. He received three full meals a day, a bunk to sleep on and a host of young men for buddies and comrades-in-arm. By degrees, his unit specialized in advanced strenuous exercises and drilled for sniper combat. Between courses, recruits were put on fatigue duty. *Life is good in this place,* opined Hugh.

On February 7, 1944, Hugh was on fatigue, detailed to the mess hall to scour pots and pans, mountains of them. Eyeing the enormous pile of work, his spirit screamed it's protest, and seeing his buddy nearby, Hugh touched his arm. "It's my birthday. Come on, George, let's celebrate!" The two sprinted from the mess hall to the barracks, exchanged their military uniforms for civies, prevailed upon another friend to join them, jumped into a parked car and were off.

The trio, free as birds, had no destination in mind, until George mentioned his sister in Montreal.

"Let's go to Montreal," the three exclaimed in unison. Alas! Their gas tank ran out near the train water station, a few miles from the army base. The boys pushed the car into nearby bushes and headed for the coal tender. They scaled the ladder by turns, then lay flat on their backs atop the coal. No one suspected there were three soldiers on the train's coal bin. The youths fell silent, then, dozed off. They didn't realize the tender had a large, funnel shaped lower area which emptied the coal slowly and evenly through the stoker and into the furnace.

Night descended upon the sleepers. Their bed of coal rocked and shifted as a mattress when one turned in sleep. An onlooker would have envied their healthy air and peaceful repose.

Of a sudden, a scream pierced the air.

"Help! Help! Get me out of here! Help."

George chose the spot where the coal was drawn into the hopper. He was unable to pull himself from the shifting, downward spiral. The heated coal became unbearable. The other two friends could not help George. They joined him in his screaming and added loud banging along the funneled shape. At intervals they pulled at George and clawed at the coal to keep him from the threads of a huge screw, which kept the coal moving downward.

When time seemed to have stopped, George seemed lost forever and his pals stood helpless, the train came to a halt. An angry fireman pulled George from the coal car with a warning to the three, never to ride a train unless seated in a coach. They had arrived at Rivière du Loup, Quebec. Undaunted by their recent experience, they stood on the main highway, hoping for a ride to Montreal. George's sister would open her house to them.

CHAPTER 11

It was late afternoon when the soldiers found the house. Hugh didn't want to return to the base. He realized he would face punishment if AWOL for less than 21 days and Court Marshall, if over 21 days. The reason for the latter being, the misdemeanor became a criminal act. In the meantime, he would find a job as he had little money.

Jobs were scarce in 1944, and pay was low. Every morning Hugh set out from the house in search of work. With two dollars in his pocket, he whistled his way toward downtown Montreal, checking every poster and paper on billboards, posts or windows.

A bright, warm sun would have boosted Hugh's expectations of finding a job, but it was February, snow fell and it was cold. Luck was on his side as he approached the town square. There, less than 100 feet from the printing press, stood a small kiosk used by paper boys to shelter their precious papers from snow and rain. A youth of 12 years was busy snipping bindings from large paper bundles. As Hugh approached, the lad, preoccupied and annoyed, accosted him.

"Jimmy's supposed to be here working. Who are you? Don't suppose you'd take his place selling, would you?"

"Funny you should ask. I need a job, any job. I'm stuck here in Montreal without money. I'd be happy to sell for you."

Placing a pack of papers on his left arm, Hugh held high one paper in his right hand shouting, "Papers, Papers! Read all about the

Canadian boys on the war front! Papers, Papers!"

His voice carried loud and clear on the airwaves, enticing eager readers to buy papers as they hurried on their way. Hugh encouraged the 12 year old to do as he had done and to use his line of shouting. The young fellow beamed when people lined up to buy papers from him.

"You made my day," he said, handing Hugh the money, he would have given Jimmy. "Hope you get a good job."

Hugh thanked him and pocketed the money thinking, *This will pay for a few meals. If only I can find a long-term job. Mom, please help me,* he prayed.

Walking along in front of the Mount Royal Hotel, Hugh saw a card in the center of a door window. It read:

Cook Assistant required

Apply inside.

Thanks, Mom, breathed Hugh as he opened the door.

CHAPTER 12

A red faced chef raised his eyes from the cake he was decorating, as Hugh stepped into the kitchen.

"Any experience?" he inquired.

"I can wash dishes, sweep and clean floors, keep things looking tidy."

"Get that apron on. Take the broom and mop from the closet behind the stove and get this mess cleaned up," barked the cook.

"Yes, Sir," responded Hugh as he headed behind the massive black cook stove occupying a third of the hotel kitchen space. Grabbing the broom, he set to work sweeping the terrazzo floor, raising a cloud of dust at each stroke.

"Stop!" shouted the cook. "You're disturbing the dust. Sweep gently and when you've finished, use the mop and a bucket of water."

"Yes Sir!" answered Hugh, catching himself from clicking his heels and saluting as learned in the drill hall.

The mop and pail of sudsy water restored the terrazzo's original luster. Hugh tackled the two kitchen windows after the floor passed inspection, then the closet after the windows.

The cook had a pleased look when Hugh completed his tasks. In a milder tone of voice he asked, "Have you eaten yet?"

"No, Sir," came the reply.

"Make yourself toast while I fry up a couple of eggs and bacon. Get some milk from the ice box, if you don't drink coffee."

"Thank you, Sir. I appreciate that," as he retrieved the milk and toasted the bread. He was famished and wolfed down the food.

There were dishes in the sink waiting to be washed and pots to scour and clean. Hugh's job kept him busy, earning him a fair wage. He was beginning his second month as kitchen assistant. Life was good, albeit a bit monotonous, until one special day—.

It happened the room service waiter wasn't at work, nor had he called in sick so no one was called to replace him. Flustered, the chef called for Hugh.

"You've got three minutes to tidy up, put on a clean cap and apron, and carry this tray to room 911."

Hugh never carried a tray so large! It was piled high with cups, saucers, plates, a pot of tea, an assortment of juices, orange sections, eggs, Danish pastries, utensils and glasses. It took a few attempts to balance the tray high on one hand, as he had seen waiters do, while keeping the other free to press the elevator button. His face lighted up as he waited for his lift to floor nine.

Elevators, in Aldershot, were rare, heavy, and pokey, if compared to the swift Montreal ones. As the door opened, Hugh stepped inside and pressed the floor number. The door closed and the elevator shot up, sending Hugh tripping forward and his tray flying high. Chinaware, glass, tea and food flew in every direction, leaving streams of liquid and globs of food on ceiling, walls and floor. Hugh picked himself up, brought the car to the main floor and hurried to get a broom, mop, and pail to clean the mess. Looking ahead as he ran toward the broom closet, he espied the chef rushing toward him, brandishing a heavy meat cleaver. The menacing look on the chef's face altered Hugh's intent. He stopped, spun around, and went rushing out the door and behind a row of low rose bushes, where he squatted to catch his breath. He peered around his rose shelter, in time to see his pursuer retreating to the kitchen. Breathing a sigh of relief, Hugh stepped from his hiding place, into a small park. He sat on a bench facing the morning sun and thought, *I'll lie low while I figure out what to do next.*

Thoughts of his foolishness and impetuosity in leaving the base, raced through his mind. These were replaced by the image of a beautiful blond girl he met one month after enlisting. He recalled receiving his first army pay and being confronted by various thoughts on how best spend it. On his day off he hopped on the recreational army vehicle going into Kentville. There, he took in a movie, spent an hour at the pool hall, ate a good dinner at Lenihan's restaurant, then walked to the Old Mill Stream, just to check out the smelt. He stood looking at the water. *What peace and calm,* he thought, *no wonder I fished here so often. Isn't it nice, Mom?*

It was time to get back to the post office and meet the base vehicle. As he stood waiting, a young woman, Theda Sandford, stopped beside him.

"Do you see that blond girl over there? She wants to meet you." The young girl introduced him to Leona McDow, her cousin. The recreational car arrived but the two arranged to meet in the same place the following week.

Hugh could not believe his good fortune. All week long he walked on air, and wondered what such a beautiful girl saw in him. He was back in Kentville every week on his day off.

How could I have been so inconsiderate as to leave the base without telling her? I didn't even think about how much I'd miss her. The stress of the pursuit, the burden of losing his job and his sadness at perhaps losing his best friend, weighed heavily on the young soldier. He was not angry, rather he felt overwhelmed and fell asleep.

CHAPTER 13

Evenings were cool in mid-March. Hugh slept several hours on the bench. He woke feeling cold, confused, until the realization of the morning's drama activated his awareness and he jumped to his feet. *So much for planning my next move,* he mused, as he started walking toward George's sister's house, his usual sleeping place. Thoughts of being labeled a deserter, if he didn't turn himself in to the Military Police, forced Hugh to make concrete plans for returning to the army.

If I go to the police now, I'll face jail and detention, not a deserter's discharge. I've been AWOL 38 days; there's only one day left. I'll pack my stuff and turn myself in tomorrow, he determined.

On the 39th and his final day on the lam, Hugh turned his steps toward the area he'd seen the military police patrol.

"I've been AWOL for 39 days but I'm ready to return to the base," he said as he approached a couple of stern looking police. The officers looked at the youthful face.

"Get lost, kid. Don't bother us with your nonsense."

"It's the truth. Phone headquarters in Aldershot," pleaded Hugh. They made the call.

Then, "Hold that man at all costs. We've been looking for him, over a month," came the order.

Hugh was taken into custody, put on trial, and sentenced to 60 days in jail. His friend, George, was apprehended and received a similar sentence. Both soldiers were dispatched to Windsor, Nova Scotia, to serve their time.

The jail was comprised of several blocks of cells, each cell fitted with iron barred doors equipped with security locks. Hugh was assigned to a cell in the front of the institute; George to a cell at the back. Mr. Duncan was the jailer and Mrs. Duncan cooked the meals. The Duncans were kind to the prisoners. Hugh was permitted the use of Mr. Duncan's workshop and tools to work on a meter long model of the famous "Blue Nose" sailing ship. Mrs. Duncan shopped for material, then sewed sails for the ship.

As Hugh worked alone on his project, George and another prisoner revealed to him their plans of escape. Would Hugh go with them? Hugh thought of Leona. He looked forward to the day of his release but would not advance it one hour and jeopardize his chance of being with Leona.

"No, George, I don't want to escape. I have one week left. I can wait."

George's comrade, an older seasoned prisoner, told George, "Hugh must die. He will inform the jailer of our plans."

"He won't squeal on us. Do you want a murder on your head? Leave him alone! We'll break out as planned, or have you forgotten how to pick locks?"

"As soon as it's dark, we're out of here. If we're caught, you'll pay with your life," threatened the other. The breakout went as planned. The two were caught the next day as they thumbed a ride back to freedom.

Hugh worked hard on his boat and completed it. He had no money to pay a lawyer to represent him. He brought the replica of the Blue Nose to show the lawyer.

"I'd be happy to take the boat as my fees," observed the lawyer. The deal was closed with a handshake.

After his release from prison in Windsor, Hugh was returned to Aldershot to serve a 28 day military sentence. The sentence was called 'detention' and was imposed on army men to test them severely so as to keep them from future detentions. For 28 days, men were forced to focus their will on enduring hard work, lack of privacy, repetitive acts, such as, transporting bricks by means of wheelbarrows from point A to point B, unloading and reloading the bricks to take them back to point A. They had to work quickly for long hours. By quitting time they fell exhausted on their bunks. They were given three healthy meals a day, all they could eat. Each day was similar to the preceding one.

Hugh got through the 28 days without breaking. He grew to manhood, learned to discipline himself, stopped swearing and using foul language, spoke respectfully to his peers and, thereby, earned their respect.

After his 28-day ordeal, Hugh decided to leave the military. The army wanted to keep him. They recognized the degree of self-discipline he'd attained and were aware of the respect Hugh had for his peers. They offered Hugh a promotion to "corporal" with two stripes on his uniform jacket. He would be in charge of training men to be soldiers.

Hugh thought about the offer, its advantages and limitations. He needed a trade and more education. He'd been assessed as having completed grade five. He wanted to marry Leona. Marriage was serious business with heavy responsibilities. As he mulled the pros and cons of his future he prayed to his angel mother for guidance and Mom heard his plea.

A building contractor offered Hugh training in carpentry. *Thank you, Mom. I'll take carpentry during the day and get education classes at night. Training on the job will give me a salary. You're the best, Mom!* he thought. So it happened.

Hugh resigned from the military. He got his journeyman ticket in three and a half years and his grade 12 equivalency in the same period.

Epilogue

On March 14, 1946, Hugh and Leona eloped. Both were 18 and neither wanted to wait any longer. They had three lovely children and 46 good years of marriage. Cancer took Leona from Hugh in May, 1992.

The couple had been married 3 years, when Hugh re-enlisted in 1949. He went into the Royal Canadian School of Engineers, both to upgrade his education and to improve his take-home cheque.

He was sent on peace-keeping duty in Korea in 1952-53 and in Cyprus in 1965-66. In Korea, Hugh lost hearing in one ear when his tank-tractor was blown up patrolling the front lines.

In 1953, fearing he would not see his family again, Hugh sent a special note to his children and included it in Leona's letter. The following is Hugh's message in full:

Guardian Angel

"Ever since I was a little boy, I've had the feeling I was not going through life on my own. I have always felt there was another dimension beyond me to whom I could turn in times of need, or to thank when things went well for me.

When I was very young I thought this other dimension was my mother who died when I was five years old. I didn't think of mother as

46

gone because I felt she had become an angel and she was watching over me from Heaven.

During my growing years I had many thought discussions in my mind with my angel mother and most always, the troubling things seemed to somehow turn out all right. It was then only proper to thank my angel mother.

Now as I look back over the years and note all the things I have gotten through and the many good things given to me, I can't help but believe I had divine help many times to get me to where I am today.

When I got older I realized I was right about my angel. That was only part of the story. The many ways in which God looks after us can only be learned through a study of the stories of Jesus in the Bible.

The enclosed pin is a reminder. You, too, have a guardian angel and for the rest of the story, the true story, please read your Bible."

The pin was a tiny figure of an angel to remind the children of God's gift of a personal guardian angel to watch over them.

Between 1960 and 1962, Hugh spent four 17 week assignments in the Canadian North West, as foreman of works in the Royal Canadian Engineers. His most gratifying work period comprised digging through the permafrost layer to lay water pipes for the military base near Whitehorse, Yukon Territories. Every year the pipes froze and people were without water. Hugh wrapped coils of electric cables around the pipes, protecting them against the frigid cold and ensuring there would be running water.

Hugh resigned from the Military in 1972. Today, he joins his fellow servicemen at the various functions and is proud to wear the nine Service Medals he earned during his many years of service to his Country. Hugh is a hero, who risked his life to keep Canada free.

After leaving the Military, Hugh joined the Saskatchewan Department of Labour as Officer of Trades and Civil Engineer Technologist. He set exams for multiple levels of trade, met with advisory boards and recommended changes to trade school personnel. Hugh worked with the schools for 15 months, then, joined the Department of Health as Senior Construction Officer. For 13 years he assisted Saskatchewan hospitals to get approval for building projects and government grants to complete them.

Hugh entered into retirement for a well-earned rest and time to enjoy a life of leisure, in 1985. He is an avid, successful golfer, with numerous trophies to display.

Photographs

Aldershot School
(Hugh Atwell is first left on the second front row)

Theda Harding
(Theda introduced Leona to Hugh)

Leona McDow
(Leona at age 17)

Hugh Atwell
(Hugh at age 16)

Hugh Atwell
(Hugh at age 17)

Hugh Atwell
(Peacekeeping in Korea)

Hugh and brother, Dempsey

Hugh Atwell
(Hugh in middle front line at a Veterans' celebration)

Hugh Atwell
(Hugh showing off one of his many trophies)

Printed in the United States
49403LVS00003B/214-417